PRINCIPLES OF STYLE
SARAH ANDREWS

This book belongs to

. . . .

A guide to creating authentic and beautiful spaces,
that can be used by you, wherever you are. Anywhere and
everywhere – or maybe somewhere one day.

PRINCIPLES OF STYLE

SARAH ANDREWS

PHOTOGRAPHY BY MARNIE HAWSON &
ANTONELLA MACHET

A JULIE GIBBS BOOK
for

New York · Amsterdam/Antwerp · London · Toronto · Sydney · New Delhi

Dearest Reader, this book was written for you.
May it guide the inner beauty you carry to your world around.

Table of Contents. INTRODUCTION 01

10 RULES OF STYLING 05

1. Curves speak of life 07
2. The triangle is a powerful figure 17
3. It's important to be different 29
4. Think about textures and layers 41
5. Focus on the unexpected 55
6. A place contains stories 67
7. Look for balance 81
8. The visible and the invisible 95
9. Eyelash testing 111
10. Use colour 123

4 HOUSES 135

Captains Rest 137
Captains Cottage 153
The Nun's Room 165
Ethelmont Rise 175

10 ROOMS 189

PLACES AND PEOPLE 210
ABOUT THE AUTHOR 213
ACKNOWLEDGEMENTS 215

INTRODUCTION

Dear Reader, how wonderful it is to be able to distil my life, teachings and experiences down into this book. May it inspire and guide you to create beautiful work around you that reflects who you are, as my school has done for so many others around the world.

My approach to design and styling has been shaped both by my education in the sciences and design, but also by my life, which has been – so far – thankfully, a big one. I started off my professional life after a childhood in remote Western Australia riding bareback on horses, swimming in azure blue seas surrounded by books and maps and encyclopedias, dreaming of all the faraway places I might visit one day as, unsurprisingly, a spatial scientist. A scientist of space and location and understanding and explaining how the world works.

I loved my profession – there was something really exciting about using the logical side of my brain to make sense of the world – but eventually I needed something more than that. A good friend once said to me, 'You should be doing for a living what you love to do in your spare time.' In my case, she was only partly right – I actually wanted to find a way of bringing together all the things I was interested in. Design and aesthetics has always been such a love of mine, which I know anyone reading this can relate to, so I went back to university in my later years to study it. It didn't take me long to realise that design was science – everything I was learning was familiar to me, and not a million miles from my spatial sciences studies. Design is so often viewed as purely creative – a bit mysterious, and relying totally on inspiration. But to me, design has structure and patterns, and follows rules. I believe it's something that anyone can learn; you don't need to have a 'naturally good eye' to make something beautiful.

After I finished my design degree, I had my own little design and marketing studio for a few years, and it was here that I started to study and dabble in interiors, houses, renovations and styling – an arm of my business and life that was truly for the love of it, and would become the greatest love of my life. I tried out many of my ideas at a rundown little shack I'd bought on the west coast of Tasmania which, even though frustratingly difficult to get to, went on to become one of the most successful and iconic Airbnbs on the planet, in a part of the world where I was told that it couldn't be done.

Emails started to trickle in from people wanting me to help them do what I had done, and I started consulting. The trickle turned into a deluge, and that's when my scientist's brain kicked in again. I realised that for everyone who was hiring me, I was essentially taking them through the same process again and again, partly around storytelling and partly around some of those rules of styling I had devised. And so I created a system that could be modified and adapted, unendingly, always producing rare and unique results.

My clients were so interested in my work and process that I developed the information into a masterclass. This brought so much success to the students who dived into it that I then set up an online school that now teaches people around the world.

This book gives a small part of my teachings to you, part art, part science – ten simple rules to guide you to create your own spaces that are uniquely yours and authentically beautiful.

My greatest joy is the fact that some of the spaces I'm going to show you are the homes of my students, with my teachings applied to them. It is a pleasure to feature them alongside my work and the work of so many I admire.

The power is yours to create a space that is beautiful to be in and is well and truly yours. As far as I'm concerned, what's beautiful is what's natural, and what's natural is what's real. If you can get to the heart of what's real for you – the truth of your story – that is unbridled, undeniable beauty. I'd really love to see what you come up with. Reach

INTRODUCTION

out to me and share the work you create from this book; it would bring me boundless joy to see the magic you make and know your story too.

I've made a map to get you from where you are to where you want to be, leaving plenty of room for mischief and magic. Magic, after all, is just science unexplained.

PART ONE

10 Rules of Styling

Anyone can create their own beautiful spaces – it's a skill we can all learn. I now know this from teaching thousands of students the world over, some of whom started out terrified and paralysed with self doubt. I'm excited to be able to share a small part of my teachings with you – ten rules of styling that can help you build a more, sensitive world around you that suits the way you'd like to live. One that's completely your own.

Rule One

CURVES SPEAK OF LIFE

In the natural world around us, you'll see lots of curves – the outer trunk of a tree, birds' eggs and feathers, clouds and waves. There are straight lines, too, but they're definitely outnumbered by curves.

If you look at the rule in terms of design on a more general level, someone who really understood the power of curves, and the way they can work with straight lines, was the industrial designer Raymond Loewy. He managed to make even the most mundane object beautiful, but he's probably best known for his designs for cars, trains, planes and even spacecraft – all sleek and streamlined, but amazingly curvaceous as well.

Somewhere along the line, decoration, age, signs of wear and the curved form started to get downplayed in many modern houses, and lines and angles began to be the hero. I have a bit of a theory that lines and angles are cheaper to build, and hence they became the norm. I bought the house I live in now for three reasons. The first is that it sits on the edge of the sea – sheltered in a way that the calm water tends to bring me peace. The second is that there's so much natural forest around it that I could always wonder at, with its changing forms and colours in different seasons and light. The third, because not a single wall here has a corner; all the bricks are laid so the rooms are rounded, and each doorway, big and small, is an arch.

Curves, in the natural world and in the spaces around us, make us feel human, comfortable, safe. They don't need to be a part of your space to begin with to have this effect on you: you can introduce them, and you'll be surprised how welcoming it will start to feel – circular rugs, round lights and coffee tables. Much more subtle curves help even more – the rounded arm of an old chair, the slightly curved spine of second-hand hardback books, a folded blanket. And of course, natural objects themselves, such as branches, dried grasses, pebbles and whatever else you can find. Proportion doesn't come into it – just because you have an enormous rectangular window doesn't mean you have to match that equally with curves. Try to balance the ratio of curves to straight in your home for a harmonious feeling.

DUNMORE FARM, MOLYULLAH, AUSTRALIA

Imperfection makes us feel human. Gentle movement, and elements that are twisted, folded and frayed, make us feel at home. I love the knots in the fabric, the rounded table legs, the old books and windswept branches against the timber boards. Imagine a plain white wall with a roller blind – it wouldn't look nearly as beautiful.

10 RULES OF STYLING

EXPERIMENT 1:

An object, no matter how humble, takes on a level of grandeur when it's standing on a column. Even a small pile of books starts to look special when it's elevated and given a certain status on this square column.

10 RULES OF STYLING

9

Experiment 2:
Let's see if we can improve things with a round column. I far prefer this look – for
me, the curve brings a sense of grace, whereas there's a rigidity to the square column.
Both options are beautiful, and both have their place; it's all a matter of taste.

10 RULES OF STYLING

LOCANDA DEL LOGGIATO, BAGNO VIGNONI, ITALY

These pages Dating back to 1300, this locanda is so welcoming. It's partly the curves in the furniture, but you can also see the hands over time in the plasterwork and hand-hewn timber. In the kitchen, a simple arch and a round table brings a storybook elegance to the room. There's nothing pretentious about anything here – it's all so honest and authentic.

Château de Dirac, Dirac, France

Overleaf This space is not intimidating at all. Although it's grand, it's brought down to such a human and comfortable level through the addition of curves – in the plants, the inexpensive wicker baskets, straw brooms and the surprising mix of unmatched chairs. The owners have done such a beautiful fit-out with really simple, humble, natural materials.

DUNMORE FARM, MOLYULLAH, AUSTRALIA

Unlike those in the Northern Hemisphere, Australian farmhouses were often constructed quickly for utilitarian purposes rather than forever. The owners of Dunmore Farm have done such a beautiful job of adding imperfection, shape and life to a bedroom in the unpretentious house through the curve of the curtains, the sweep of branches by the bedside and the ceiling light.

10 RULES OF STYLING

DUNMORE FARM, MOLYULLAH, AUSTRALIA

If you try to work out why this house looks so inviting and comfortable, it's often in the subtle details, such as the lovely old skirting board against the timber weatherboard walls.

It's obvious that the owners of this house have put it together so carefully and lovingly, and they're using pieces that have meaning for them and that tell of their story.

Rule Two

THE TRIANGLE IS
A POWERFUL FIGURE

While you're flicking though the pages of this book, and see a room or a vignette that feels pleasing to your eye, always stop and consider why that might be. Your answers will help you add to this book of principles. A good place to start considering what you find visually beautiful is geometry.

It can be really overwhelming trying to arrange your belongings in a space until you realise that certain patterns can help you tie it all together. The triangle, in particular, is what I'm talking about here. Creating high points and low points has been sage advice from stylists, florist and artists of any types – and was one of the first styling rules I learnt that has never really failed me. When you've collected everything in one spot, have a go at assembling it into triangles of various shapes and sizes. There's no need to be too literal about it – these aren't necessarily all simple, basic, straight triangles; they can be a lot looser than that. What you should be aiming for are high points and low points and making everything feel beautiful, relaxed and not overly thought out. At the back, you'll have large triangles, with smaller triangles closer to the front. On shelves and flat surfaces, think about the triangle as you make little compositions – feathers or well-used paintbrushes grouped together in a jar, for instance. By the time you're finished, you'll have layer upon layer of triangles. It's about creating rhythm and interest, so your eye can move from one object to the next, and take things in gradually.

LUCY'S LANE, PORT FAIRY, AUSTRALIA

Sarah did an online course of mine, and I've assigned her an A+ for her ability to arrange objects in triangles. She's brought a lovely old stone cottage from the 1860s back to life – it used to be part of a dairy farm – and has done such a beautiful job throughout the house.

Experiment 1:

Don't be afraid of spaces; they just contain a collection of objects
you live with. Chairs, tables, lamps, art, memories. It's about the things
you love – it's your home after all.

10 RULES OF STYLING

19

EXPERIMENT 2:
The most comfortable way to put things together, I think, is with one high point and two low ones. Even though the first experiment looks good, the addition of the two tiles, which I chose because I liked the colour, makes the space feel finished to me.

10 RULES OF STYLING

LE MOULIN BRÉGEON, LINIÈRES-BOUTON, FRANCE

These pages These rooms in an 18th-century converted watermill in the Loire Valley demonstrate textbook flawless styling, elevated by the timber beam. Beautiful objects tell their story simply, placed in triangles. It looks uncontrived because it's been done with an amazing eye; any of these objects in any other arrangement wouldn't look as good.

ALBERT AND GRACE, BOONAH, AUSTRALIA

Overleaf Cheryl Carr, a dear friend who assists me at my classes, has restored a deconsecrated church in Queensland and has done such a lovely job of it. Her ability to collect, curate and arrange, quite seriously hundreds of objects is so impressive. Everything always looks perfect as she arranges it all, in small groups and collectively overall, in triangles.

10 RULES OF STYLING

24

FOLLONICO, MONTEFOLLONICO, ITALY

These pages Two rooms in a Tuscan country house show the power of a few simple things placed perfectly – in an alcove, a cupboard and a wine basket, along with a few objects on top of the cupboard; in the bedroom, a chair, a light and a bed. As an exercise, switch the light and chair in your mind and you'll see that it wouldn't have that same simple beauty.

10 RULES OF STYLING

LUCY'S LANE, PORT FAIRY, AUSTRALIA

Overleaf My student Sarah shows that sometimes all a space needs is one perfect thing, and in this setting, by the sea, the ship couldn't be more appropriate. The dried fennel flower and banksia are added in the correct place to enhance the triangle and give life and movement to the arrangement. Sarah definitely gets top marks from me again for this.

Rule Three

IT'S IMPORTANT TO BE DIFFERENT

In an increasingly globalised world, it's still quite easy to find clues about how people in various countries live, and how different that is from the way we do. It's those signs that we notice when we're travelling or that a spatial scientist can use to help build up a picture of how a place works: the neat rows of shoes inside the front door in Japanese apartments makes me think of order and structure; the packed parking stations for bicycles in Belgian towns remind me of that nationality's enthusiasm for community and green living; the uniform mailboxes outside houses in rural USA trigger ideas for me about culture and tradition.

Translate that to your own home – it sounds really obvious, but the easiest way to make your place memorable and comfortable is to fill it with pieces that are unique to you, and that hold meaning for you. Uniqueness creates a stamp on our memories. There are some homes we have visited – or seen in magazines or online – that we'll never forget. I dare say not too many of these would have been standard, or on trend – but instead are unique, reflecting the person who lived there.

That doesn't mean you can't look elsewhere for inspiration; it doesn't mean either that everything around you has to be handmade or custom. It's more that you take your time to put together a unique world around you that speaks of who you are and the life you live and have lived.

In the following pages I've chosen spaces that I just can't forget. Their objects and decoration feel to me to come from a place of truth of the person who put them there or chose them. I encourage all of us to ask questions of ourselves when choosing things for our homes. Do I like this? How does this make me feel? Is this special enough to live with?

FORMER HUNTING LODGE, DORSET, ENGLAND

The stag in the entrance hall was designed and modelled by Geoffrey Preston in stucco, a traditional material made from lime putty, marble dust, gypsum and glue, which was widely employed in the 18th century, but is now rarely used. I love that story, and that Geoffrey is reviving an old trade.

30

Experiment 1:

Let's see if we can create a beautiful vignette, using what we've learnt so far –
curves, triangles and something different. This looks good, but I think we may
be able to do something more interesting.

10 RULES OF STYLING

31

Experiment 2:

Let's do it again and try to make something more memorable. I know everyone has images in their minds of things they'll never forget. The key to making these memories is often the unexpected.

10 RULES OF STYLING

STELOR, GOTLANDS TOFTA, SWEDEN

Previous pages 'Blue and green should never be seen without a colour in between', as the old saying goes. However, as far as I'm concerned, it should be more like '... unless you want people to remember where they've been'. This hotel on the Swedish island of Gotland is the most Instagrammable farm stay ever. I can't wait to get there one day.

STELOR, GOTLANDS TOFTA, SWEDEN

These pages The family have collected beautiful things without fear of conforming to the expected, and, at the same time, are on a mission to celebrate what they love about Gotland – the natural beauty of the island, and their friends and neighbours who produce everything from food for the table to art for the walls. It translates to a feeling of joy and is timelessly charming.

VILLA PIENZA, PIENZA, ITALY

These pages Two sisters renovated this house in Tuscany, and it looks fantastic. Things that shouldn't work together do – the oversized swan on the wall alongside the tall bedside lamp; the wall light hanging above the artworks in the sitting room. It's so obvious to me that the sisters only used what they love, and there's a warmth and charm to the place because of it.

Maison Bergogne, Narrowsburg, USA

Overleaf This emporium in a hamlet on the Delaware River near the Catskill Mountains in New York state is one of the most magical places I know. It used to be a bus garage, but you'd never know that now – it's more like an art installation. Juliette, who named the shop in honour of her grandmother, has an incredible eye for curious objects, treasures and relics.

Rule Four

THINK ABOUT TEXTURES AND LAYERS

I've already talked about geometry, and now it's time to mention numbers – odd ones. I know this is starting to sound like a maths lesson, but bear with me! When it comes to textures and layers, I always work in odd numbers – three, five or seven. It's something to do with everything being just slightly off, which, to me, feels human. And slightly magical at the same time – many of our favourite childhood characters came in threes. The bears, musketeers and little pigs for a start.

If you work in even numbers, there's too much of a temptation to make things match. The risk then is that they end up looking predictable, or just too neat. Neat, to me, feels forgettable. As long as you have plenty of textures and layers in a space, there'll be a sense of discovery for the eyes – you'll notice different things and make new connections every time you step into it. At the other extreme, in a minimalist contemporary house, you'll probably find one artwork on the wall, a couple of pieces of furniture and a lamp, and maybe a few books on a shelf. You can take the whole room in at once, and while it might be quite dramatic at first glance, it won't really make much of a lasting impression. In a more layered approach, you'll be drawn to the space, and can spend time exploring, allowing yourself time to think, feel and understand.

Hôtel de Tingry, Ménerbes, France

The history of this house in Provence, built in the 17th century, is celebrated, not sanitised. In any other hands, the door may have been restored and the floor levelled, but they're part of life here. Even before you dwell on the beautiful fresco, you can almost sense the eras and the stories that have gone before.

Experiment 1:

Let's have a play with numbers here. Start with a collection of four beautiful objects with varying textures and a colour palette that works well together. Move them around until the arrangement looks as good as it possibly can. This is lovely, but I think we can do better.

10 RULES OF STYLING

Experiment 2:
Take one of the objects away and keep playing. To my eye, the three together look so much better and more memorable than the four. Three is the smallest number of elements you can put together to create a pattern. To me, the objects now stand out like three concise bullet points on a page and I can enjoy them.

Hôtel de Tingry, Ménerbes, France

These pages The same applies to textures as to objects – too many textures can err a little too far towards cosiness, while too few feels slightly too monastic. There's a happy number in three, five or seven. The kitchen, a utilitarian space, has fewer textures and layers than the sitting room, and that's appropriate. It's interesting to see the different approach in the two rooms.

MAISON EMPEREUR, MARSEILLE, FRANCE

Overleaf The apartment above a family-run hardware shop that opened in 1827 is all about story, furnished with pieces from the archives. Beyond that, it's also about texture and layering: the untreated timber bed and linen pillows; the slightly ornate standard lamp begging for a shade, but so much better without; the well-worn timber cabinet and exposed plumbing.

10 RULES OF STYLING

My Sister & The Sea, Marion Bay, Australia

I'm going to hand a top grade to some more students of mine for their use of textures and layers. In this humble seaside hideaway, the two sisters, who are both keen thrifters and it shows, have so lovingly created a space that really tells their story. When you love thrift shopping as much as they do, it can be easy to overdo it, but they've managed to strike just the right balance.

10 RULES OF STYLING

MY SISTER & THE SEA, MARION BAY, AUSTRALIA

The drive to this sweet little cottage on the southern tip of the Yorke Peninsula in South Australia takes in lots of little towns and villages, each with a thrift store or two. The sisters stop at each one every time. My Sister & The Sea, which is not surprisingly a really popular place to stay, is the high-tide mark for every thrift store on the way. I love the idea of that.

EWING FARM, TYLDEN, AUSTRALIA

These pages The owners of this farmhouse in Victoria, built in 1862, have retained the textures and exposed the layers. In some rooms, the shingles in the ceiling are still visible; outside the roofs are rusted and the weatherboards oiled rather than painted. It's all so unpretentious and appropriate; throughout, there's such a sense of warmth and comfort.

EWING FARM, TYLDEN, AUSTRALIA

Overleaf I love these two rooms – in the old kitchen, the painted brickwork and weatherboard, the old stove and broad floorboards, the choice of artwork and the drying rack hanging from the ceiling. And in the beautiful outdoor room, rather than making the door and windows look in perfect condition, the owners have gone in a different direction.

Rule Five

FOCUS ON THE UNEXPECTED

As a scientist, I'm constantly looking for patterns to explain how the world works, to tell a story. Part of that story is to do with things that are unexpected, that stand out and send you off on a tangent. Like the High Line in Manhattan – the beautiful and surprisingly meadow-like park on a disused elevated railway line above the streets.

That focus on the unexpected can translate into how you organise your home. You have some things to hang on the wall, objects that mean something to you, and a pile of your favourite books. The most obvious thing to do would be to space the paintings regularly at eye level, put the objects on the table and books on a shelf. But forget about the usual way – think of where you'd never see something. A painting hung where you have to bend down to look at it; books stacked in a corner of the room; shoes on a shelf.

One of the spaces I enjoy the most in my home is the pantry. You'll find everything removed from its packets and decanted into glass jars; beautiful plates and cups and far too many glasses for champagne and not enough for water; but you'll also find a pair of abalone shells, from my first ever dive for them off the coast of Tasmania where I live, a sea eagle's egg in a shallow pewter goblet, a bust of a veiled woman my mother gifted to me and my collection of incense, table candles, sage, a dried flower in a bud vase. The home I live in is old, but it is new to me. And while I slowly move into its spaces and discover how I want to live here, this little pantry brings solace that this home is mine.

Never feel like you need to subscribe to the expected; please always subscribe to the interesting and to that which feels like you.

You might worry that it will look a bit odd – you'll probably need to experiment until it feels right. Along the way, you may discover you don't have room for some bits and pieces, which can be hard. Once you've arranged your space with objects in unlikely places, you'll find that your brain will connect to them, and you'll have an immediate response, like me in my kitchen pantry – pleasure.

SIBELLA COURT, SYDNEY, AUSTRALIA

I've admired Sibella Court for years – she creates memorable spaces that feel magical to me. They're also quite playful; here, I love the giant headboard and the owl overhead. The lighting is inspired; many people would be tempted to do something grander, but Sibella knows how to make a space unforgettable.

56

EXPERIMENT 1:

I came across a formula about how to hang a picture – the centre of it had to be at around 150 cm from the floor, then you had to divide the height of the frame by two, take away the distance from the top of the frame to the hanging hardware, and add this to the 150 cm. We tried that here; it looks fine, but I think we could do better.

10 RULES OF STYLING

57

EXPERIMENT 2:

If you want everything at eye level, you need a complicated formula. But, to me, it's much more memorable when things hang at different heights and in unexpected places. The next experiment could be to move the paintings down to the lower panels to see if that looks even more interesting.

10 RULES OF STYLING

LA FUSTAIA, SARZANA, ITALY

These pages This is such a beautiful property in northern Italy, not far from La Spezia. What I love about it is that everything they've done is unexpected. The reach of the lights, the placement of the taps so far above the basin; even the way the pillows and cushion are arranged on the bed. A few things used differently enough create a space you wouldn't forget.

10 RULES OF STYLING

LA FUSTAIA, SARZANA, ITALY

Overleaf In every room there's something surprising – a few very contemporary elements mixed in with the books on the ladder, the old bicycle up in the eaves, the twisted curtain dripping into the tray on the floor and the completely informal arrangement of dried branches in the fireplace. The rooms are grown up but playful, and there's a magic to them.

10 RULES OF STYLING

SHIP INN, STANLEY, AUSTRALIA

Lynda Gardener and Belle Hemming Bright designed the interiors of this storytelling hotel in Stanley, an old port town in north-west Tasmania. When I'm at the Ship Inn, I find myself thinking of pirates, rule breakers and seafarers. Lynda and Belle break every supposed rule and, in doing so, create so many special moments; the portrait is tiny, which just makes you want to peer closer.

SHIP INN, STANLEY, AUSTRALIA

In many hotels, everything is very ordered and slightly formal; here, it's disorganised to the point of being beautiful, and that's the idea. I really love the way these cushions and pillows have been almost thrown together – it's so surprising. The wall light is far closer to the bed than you would expect it to be, which just adds to the overall charm of the place.

SIBELLA COURT, SYDNEY, AUSTRALIA

I remember when Sibella Court's first book *Etcetera* came out; it was so different from anything else that was around at the time. She has always inspired me with her ability to create a sense of joy and quiet theatre in her interiors. They're always so romantic and understated, and high end without anything in there being high end in any way.

SIBELLA COURT, SYDNEY, AUSTRALIA

Sibella's interiors are always so full of history, craft and storytelling; she can take mismatched, overlooked and often really modest pieces and create magical worlds. A complete bowerbird who finds beauty in unexpected places, Sibella has her own product ranges as well as designing some of the most memorable bars and hotels around. She's a bit of a pirate, too, and I love that.

Rule Six

A PLACE CONTAINS STORIES

When I was a student myself, I realised that there was a real narrative element to spaces that connected with me.

While I'm working on any space, be it a whole house or a small vignette, I always start with thinking about the story of it all. As humans, we are so drawn to narrative that we tell ourselves stories while we sleep. It makes sense that the spaces around us we connect best with also seem to talk to us; we instantly understand them, and how they want us to use them. This book contains four houses I worked on using story to guide me. Stories about history, place, the natural world, characters real and make-believe – often versions of myself should I exist in another place and time. When I am working for a client, I always ask myself, 'How would I want to live here?'

Of course you want beautiful things around you, but I feel that everything has to have a purpose, echoing part of the story you're trying to tell. It doesn't all have to happen immediately – think of it more like writing a novel, chapter by chapter, letting it gradually evolve over time, editing along the way.

Once you start to think this way about your spaces, they start to truly become alive – and once you wholeheartedly start to build your story around you, now you're building your own world. I cannot think of a more delightful thing.

WORMISTOUNE, CRAIL, SCOTLAND

Wormistoune, the home of the McCallum family and a place of myth and legend, is really special to me. I know the family and have been lucky enough to spend time here. I had the whole place to myself one snowy winter – I felt myself transported back to 17th-century Scotland.

EXPERIMENT 1:

We all love good stories, because we can imagine ourselves in them.
Let's experiment with some beautiful objects and see what happens.
To me, this looks as if it's setting a scene; I want it to do more than that.

10 RULES OF STYLING

69

EXPERIMENT 2:

By adding the extra elements, we're now telling the story of who's been there and experienced the space. There's a good story here that draws us into the image, makes connections and lets us tell our own stories.

10 RULES OF STYLING

STEAM, FORREST, AUSTRALIA

These pages Fleur is an outstanding student of mine, with multiple very successful properties under her belt now. She has taken the principles I taught her to heart to create some truly beautiful places that tell powerful stories to benefit both her art and business. She renovated the derelict train carriage in such a respectful way, celebrating the craftsmanship of an earlier age.

Steam, Forrest, Australia

Overleaf Set in a village in the Otway Ranges in Victoria, Fleur's restored train carriage demonstrates so many of the rules of styling. It's surprising; the curves of the carriage itself are echoed in everything from the furniture and lighting to the fan and flue. She's also managed a level of restraint – as you'll discover in a later lesson, the eye needs a rest every now and then.

Smokey Belles, Narrowsburg, USA

Right on the edge of the Catskills in New York state, Smokey Belles embraces what the Catskills are all about. It tells a very true and powerful narrative about both the region and the owner – who built the cabin from scratch – and tells it without any fuss. This is another example of restraint – it could have been tempting to cover every surface, but it's so much better with less.

SMOKEY BELLES, NARROWSBURG, USA

Here's a room that demonstrates so many rules: the use of the curve in the unusual bedhead; the simple triangle formed by the bed, picture and lamp; the subtle use of textures, layers and colours; the perfect balance shown in the space that, without all the other components, could have appeared monastic. The few carefully chosen elements add up to a well told story.

10 RULES OF STYLING

WORMISTOUNE, CRAIL, SCOTLAND

These pages There's story in every room at Wormistoune, including a ceiling that has been painted to tell the history of the house and the McCallum family. Every time I walked past it, I couldn't help looking at the image of a mother holding a baby – it's directly above where one of the sons of the present owners was born in that room. It's such a beautiful image.

WORMISTOUNE, CRAIL, SCOTLAND

Overleaf I fell in love with the McCallum tartan, which was everywhere. I had the time of my life at Wormistoune – there were secrets all through the house. I got locked in a room once, but found a secret door to get out and had to go up two levels and then down a hidden staircase – it was so wonderful and I felt I was part of the story myself for a few moments.

Rule Seven

LOOK FOR BALANCE

Tobler's first law of geography states that everything is related to everything else, but near things are more related than distant things. The closer together, the stronger the relationship; the further apart, the weaker that relationship will be. In geography, we use the law to explain relationships and meaning in the world, like why, where and when wildflowers grow.

In putting a room, or a whole house, together, it plays a role in helping us to decide what, and how much, stuff will work best. It's tempting to cover every surface with lovely things, but that can be overwhelming. It's important to be a bit restrained, so your eye can take everything in gradually, have a rest along the way, and not be bombarded by pure beauty. You want pieces that sit closer together to have a relationship, tell a story – with practice, you'll be able to find those links, which will be personal to you.

For every busy area, you'll need about the same amount of quiet – it's all about finding balance. A good rule of thumb is about 50:50, but that can vary slightly, depending on what you're trying to say in your world around you. If it is one that's full and bubbly, amp it up; if the aim is to make you feel calm, turn the dial down.

Taking stuff away is just as important, maybe more so, as putting things in. It's to do with editing – the strange thing is that too many amazing things together can have much less impact than just the right number. Again, just experiment here – I know I do.

My bedroom is a giant space that fills an entire floor and looks out to sea. It's giant because I'm the only one living here, and found the idea of empty dark rooms that I'd never use so sad I had walls taken out so the light can spill around. I spent months wondering how I might divide the space so it works best – perhaps add a library or a private sitting area … or a proper bath room. A room that just contained a bath, a beautiful spot to spend an entire evening. Eventually I realised I just want calm – to lie in bed and watch the ocean and not be drawn back into my inner world of books and business and all the inside things we do. So the space remains open, with canvas lanterns that sway in the breeze and make me feel a part of it all.

Reflect on how you want to feel in your own spaces, and use the idea of balance, either up or down, to help guide you. When you pin it down, it's a beautiful thing.

NUMEROVENTI, FLORENCE, ITALY
The owners of this apartment have succeeded in creating a peaceful retreat for travellers. Sometimes enough is enough – the temptation here would be to add an armchair or a lamp, but it just doesn't need it.

10 RULES OF STYLING

EXPERIMENT 1:

What I like to teach students is to start with 50 per cent of a space
filled with elements and 50 per cent empty, and then play with the ratios up
and down to either create calm or create a bold and charming story.

EXPERIMENT 2:

The first experiment looks a little too calm to me, but you might find it just right. Adding one more element, to me, really adds life to the setting, but still gives the eye plenty of room to rest.

10 RULES OF STYLING

VALDIROSE, LASTRA A SIGNA, ITALY

These pages Here we see in rooms at Valdirose, a 19th-century villa in the hills just outside Florence, an exquisite demonstration of how beautiful objects can just be beautiful objects, and spaces can breathe, when the eye is allowed room to rest. Take any one thing away from here and the rooms could feel spartan; as they are, there's a sense of great calm and comfort.

10 RULES OF STYLING

VALDIROSE, LASTRA A SIGNA, ITALY

Overleaf Notice the large-scale proportions of the room and the smaller proportion of a simple setting on a breakfast table – in each case, there is breathing room and everything is perfectly placed. I love it that even the tablecloth is no bigger than it needs to be – it creates its own small scene. It's such a lesson in finding just the right objects and using restraint.

THE OXFORD, HEPBURN SPRINGS, AUSTRALIA

Previous pages To me, there's nothing more beautiful than a twin room – it's all about balance and symmetry. In this one, the paintings on either side of the beds are a slightly different size and at a slightly different distance from the window, which brings life to the room. Twin rooms always remind me of staying with my grandma, and I'd sleep in the bed on the left.

BLACK SWAN INN, ST HELENS, TASMANIA

These pages My friends Amanda and Skip both have a sense for incredible objects but also of the restraint needed to be able to celebrate them. As well as showing how balance works in a space, these photos, taken mid-renovation of the old inn into a private home, also demonstrate the use of curves and triangles as well as of textures and layers, and the importance of story.

NUMEROVENTI, FLORENCE, ITALY

I've always liked that phrase 'kill your darlings' – it's an important muscle to flex. There would be a temptation to hang a few things on the wall or use the top of the cabinet as a surface to display objects, but the owners of these apartments have resisted that, and the room looks so much better for it. The cabinet is such a bold piece that it really doesn't need anything else around it.

STELOR, GOTLANDS TOFTA, SWEDEN

The grand desk feels important enough, as does the chair, that the owners haven't fussed with them. An elaborate desk setting and a framed painting in the background would almost negate the beauty of these two objects. Even in this uncluttered scene, there's an element of surprise – the artwork hangs on a trouser hanger, which is such a contrast to the elaborate furniture.

Rule Eight

THE VISIBLE AND THE INVISIBLE

It's no coincidence that certain places that are meant to make us feel safe and secure are pretty streamlined without too much extra stuff around. Think about an airport – when it comes to the check-in desk, for instance, there's really nothing to look at apart from a little digital display to tell you how much your luggage weighs. With the high barrier in front of it, you can't even usually see the desk itself, but you do get to watch your bags head off towards the plane, which is somehow reassuring. Apart from the areas where they're trying to get you to shop or eat, airports generally don't have too much on display. We're not supposed to see the workings of them; we're just supposed to feel confident that everything will work okay.

When you translate that to our homes, we all have objects that don't look great – fridge, TV, toaster, washing machine, desky things. They can all be useful, but just not that pretty. When everything is out, it can start to feel just a bit chaotic and inefficient.

It feels powerful and magical to be able to makes things in your home visible or invisible. My friends and colleagues laugh, I have a real dislike of cords, plastics and certain shades of reds and purples. But, as hard as I try, even I can't go through life without bumping into them.

Find ways of hiding things away where you can – I put my appliances in cupboards or behind doors or curtains. A living room looks much better, I think, if the TV is tucked away in a cabinet rather than being this dirty great thing hanging on the wall. You get a pass if it's something you use all day long, but these days I prefer to watch a movie in bed on my laptop. Shove all your desky things in a drawer or box if you can – handy but not in full view all the time. Mine go in tiny baskets, one for pens, one for cords etc. It's nice to feel relaxed when you open hidden spaces. One of my students pointed out when I showed her my cupboards, 'It's like it's living its best Pinterest life!' I love thinking about it like that and, of course, with the cupboards in my own home and certain spaces (we all have them), I just try to avoid eye contact with them.

CAMELLAS-LLORET, MONTRÉAL, FRANCE
A single thing out of place or out of keeping, such as a coloured bedspread or a black lamp, would distract you and completely destroy the simple beauty of this bedroom in a small guesthouse near Carcassonne.

Experiment 1:

It's unavoidable that we need to live with practical things, but I always try to hide them in any way I can. This cord at ground level is fairly inconspicuous, but I'd rather it disappeared altogether.

EXPERIMENT 2:

Remember the earlier lesson about putting objects in unexpected places –
that's very useful here. Some old books in an unlikely spot conceal the cord;
true inspiration and creativity come out when there's a challenge.

10 RULES OF STYLING

Château de Dirac, Dirac, France

These pages Kitchens and other functional spaces are hotspots for ugly objects such as plastic spatulas, appliance cords and Tupperware containers, but the owners of this ancient château have demonstrated that you can find and display beautiful alternatives to these objects, and hide the rest in creative ways. Notice the bamboo rod holding up the curtain under the sink.

THE BUTCHER'S HOUSE, BOTHWELL, AUSTRALIA

Overleaf Vanessa studied with me when she first bought this old cottage. It's steeped in Tasmanian Noir, having once been a butchery. She's done such a beautiful job at curating this perfectly – the place is imperfect, and everything she's chosen for it is humble and beautiful and considered. There's a calm in that the modern signs of life have been hidden away; there's nothing jarring here.

10 RULES OF STYLING

The Butcher's House, Bothwell, Australia

These pages I'm awarding a high distinction to Vanessa for the work she has done on her house. Since graduating, she's done very well with this iconic Tasmanian property, and I'm not surprised – by embracing the story of the house, visitors feel as if they're transported back to a darker time in the island's history, and by concealing unattractive modern necessities, they are able to linger there.

10 RULES OF STYLING

THE BUTCHER'S HOUSE, BOTHWELL, AUSTRALIA

Overleaf This is such a humble space and, again, Vanessa has done it so well. The kitchen almost seems freestanding which, in this case, tends to make an appliance like the fridge disappear. It's tucked away as much as possible anyway, and there are enough beautiful objects around to distract your attention. This is also a lesson in balance, textures and layers.

CAMELLAS-LLORET, MONTRÉAL, FRANCE

These pages This property just speaks to the curation of only the most necessary and beautiful things. Their eye for large and small scale beauty is impressive. What's unnecessary is in the eye of the beholder – some people would be tempted to hide the flowerpots away, but adding the unexpected bust elevates them into something quite special and brings story.

NAPIER QUARTER, FITZROY, AUSTRALIA

Overleaf This room by Daniel, one of my students and a friend, is about not doing too much – really beautiful simple curtains, a grand mirror and one chair, uncluttered by some of the necessities of life. With buildings like this, people often go crazy and fill the space, but Daniel puts things together so confidently, which is possible when you're only using things you love.

Rule Nine

EYELASH TESTING

I can't help thinking about old-style shopping malls when I talk about why this rule makes sense to me. They're my idea of a nightmare, with all their bright lights, clashing colours, lack of fresh air, illogical layouts and different music coming from all over the place. Some people love them, and that's absolutely fine – it's great that we're all different. All the things I don't like about shopping centres are there for a reason – they've been designed to make us feel slightly disoriented, lose track of time and put us in the mood to spend money on things we don't necessarily need. They heighten all our senses. I recently discovered there is a term for this – sensory sensitivity. And I found that people who tend to make the most beautiful delicate considered spaces also suffer from it, so I don't feel alone in this.

Spaces like this wouldn't pass what I've officially called 'the eyelash test', which is a clever and really easy way of finding out what's working and what's not in the spaces you create. One thing I really love about this rule is it works almost on a subconscious level. Once I've styled a space and feel that it's almost there, I'll squint and see what colours are popping out and looking out of place. It's funny, but it's usually reds and yellows that are the offenders – colours that in nature often signal danger. Having said that, though, I'm sometimes really surprised by what jumps out – it can be something really small and beautiful, that you don't really notice when your eyes are open. It's amazing how much better the space will look without it, though. I'll do the eyelash test several times until the space is calm and still, and I can see that it just looks right.

VILLA 61, LIMANA, ITALY

Doing the eyelash test doesn't mean you're left with a monochromatic or bland scheme; it means you're left with a scheme that works. Going back to earlier rules, this room speaks of curves, balance and texture.

EXPERIMENT 1:

There isn't a single thing that isn't beautiful in this image, but using my eyelash test on it, the two colours of red in the couch and flower clash. To me, it would be better without one of them.

EXPERIMENT 2:

Removing the flower and replacing it with the ball instantly elevates the space to one that feels considered and balanced. If I had a vase of different blooms on hand, it could be a completely different story.

The Waterfront House, Erowal Bay, Australia

These pages My student Elizabeth gets top marks for mastering the eyelash test at her house on the New South Wales south coast – nothing jars in the least. She's done a beautiful job on the whole house and used many of the lessons learnt while studying with me. She told me after class that I'd found the secret and it was so generous of me to share it – I found that very touching.

10 RULES OF STYLING

THE COTTAGE, KANGAROO VALLEY, AUSTRALIA

Overleaf Artist and stylist Lisa Madigan curated the interior of her 1880s cottage in country New South Wales. It used to house the local newspaper and is so full of story and interest. She inspires me – she's so masterful in the objects she puts together and the palettes she chooses. Everything in this room is entirely appropriate, giving it such a sense of calm.

10 RULES OF STYLING

118

CHÂTEAU D'UZER, UZER, FRANCE

These pages These two rooms in a château in the Ardèche region of France have no trouble at all passing the eyelash test. They're two really special spaces, and what makes them memorable is the element of surprise – in one room, the huge sun on the fireplace which almost mirrors the floor tiles and, in the other, the life-size sheep standing in front of the table.

Villa 61, Limana, Italy

Overleaf The eyelash test has been taken to the nth degree in this Veneto guesthouse, and the result is so elegant. In other hands, it might have been plain and boring. But it's the wildflowers placed in varying humble vessels and, unexpectedly, just loose on the table; the half tablecloth and the balance of textures and layers – it's so, so beautiful.

Rule 10

USE COLOUR

It's only in recent years I've become a lover of colour. Before that, in a sense I think I was too young to be brave enough to use it. What a powerful thing – some shades of red have a strong enough effect on me to make me turn away, while I can look at some shades of pink in the evening sky that move me so deeply I feel an ache that can only be located in the exact spot my heart is.

Be brave, too, and don't wait as long as I did. I was thinking the other day, ask any little kid what their favourite colour is and they'll give you a very definite answer. Mine was pink. What was yours? When did you forget it? For me, I can trace it back to when I started to open magazines and books and noticed every single house was white. 'Oh,' I learnt, 'houses are supposed to be white.'

When you're putting a space together, I know it feels safe to go for a neutral colour. But you'll end up with a room that's forgettable in every way. I don't think that's why we're here. We are here to create rooms and spaces that are beautiful, memorable and entirely our own. Colour moves how we think and feel, so start there. Experiment – you might not get it right first time, but that's all right. Colour has nothing to do with trends or fashion – it's something that's deep within each of us, highly personal and completely individual.

Remember to celebrate the shades you fall in love with, the ones that tug at your heart a little bit and you won't ever forget. That delicate pink you find in skies for me. I'm a lover of old-rope brown, decaying-fishing-buoy creams, Italian terracotta and the greens you find on old enamels. What about you?

AURÉLIE ALVAREZ, L'ISLE SUR LA SORGUE, FRANCE

This is Aurélie Alvarez's studio in the rafters of her 16th-century home. I just love the use of colour in her works, which explore the duality between science and spirituality. She combines colours that you'd never think of putting together – it really inspires me to experiment and try the unexpected.

124

EXPERIMENT 1:

Colour is the most powerful and effective way to communicate and can create instant story. Let's try this first with minimal colour; the three chairs look lovely together – the power of three – but, to my mind, just a little too quiet.

EXPERIMENT 2:

Adding a coloured chair, for me, creates a moment I want to dwell on rather than appreciate and move quickly by. It's playful, but the interesting thing is that if you added a second coloured chair, it would dilute the effect of just one.

10 RULES OF STYLING

LA BELLE VUE, NEFFIÈS, FRANCE

These pages I often spend winters here with my friends who own this B&B in Languedoc-Roussillon in southern France, and it's so good to have the time to appreciate their home. Their use of colour – the pinks and the greys – makes this place special and their own. Colour doesn't have to be bold to make an impact; here, it ties the spaces together in a really gentle way.

Aurélie Alvarez, L'Isle sur la Sorgue, France

Overleaf I couldn't resist showing you more of Aurélie Alvarez's works. It's so easy to get lost in the colours, textures and patterns she creates – they're just so beautiful. Look for inspiration wherever you can find it – it would be so interesting and inspiring to use one of her works as a starting point for a room, just to see what would happen.

10 RULES OF STYLING

L'ÉPICERIE DE VÉNAT, SAINT-YRIEIX-SUR-CHARENTE, FRANCE

These pages The colour is the hero here – the bold use of green is so wonderful and joyous, and creates a space that's really professional despite being one that's put together with collected and quite humble objects. Green is used throughout the B&B, but not always in exactly the same shade, which gives a different experience of the effect of colour.

L'épicerie de Vénat, Saint-Yrieix-sur-Charente, France

Overleaf The building, which housed a grocery store, coffee shop and post office for many years before being abandoned, has been brought back to life through exuberant colour and an individual and unexpected mix of vintage objects, include retro toys and games. As well as being a B&B, it's kept its grocery origins, with jars of jam and bottles of wine lined up on shelves.

PART TWO

4 Houses

Now we have learnt the basics, let me show you how it's all applied. Let me show you around four houses that mean a lot to me – they're all places I've lived in, or loved, one way or another.

Places I've created or helped put together; and ones I've spent years or months in. They all feel like home to me. Who says home can only be one place?

I grew up on a windswept beach at the end of the world, which is probably where my love of boats came from. I'd look out to sea and dream of faraway, lonely islands full of ghosts and treasures and birds I had never seen, but wanted to one day. Even as a little kid, I was an escape artist – as soon as I could walk, I was off. When I was nine months old, I climbed out of my crib and out the front door. By the time my mum spotted me a few streets away, she said I just turned around, waved and kept on going. I've kept on escaping ever since, in one way or another.

A few years ago, I realised it was time for another escape – after my dreams of sailing around the world came to an end when I was shipwrecked off the Mexican coast, I eventually landed back in Australia. I ended up owning my own design and marketing business, which was successful, but I was doing work I wasn't in love with. I was living in a town that I wasn't in love with, and in a marriage that I wasn't in love with either. I needed a getaway. Flicking through a magazine one day, I came across a ramshackle holiday shack up for sale in a remote spot on the west coast of Tasmania, far far away from where I was living at the time.

Clinging to the water's edge, this tiny hut was like a boat hauled up onto the shore, a lovely mix of everything that's important to me. I didn't even bother to go and look at it – I somehow knew it was what I needed, a safe harbour, and bought it immediately.

When I finally made my way there, I discovered it was pretty derelict – doors and windows hanging off the hinges, no electricity or running water, a total mess. I didn't even need a key to get in, as the whole place was wide open. For a few days, I was completely overwhelmed, spent quite a bit of time crying and wondering what I'd got myself into, not just with this place, but in my life in general. Eventually I pulled up my bootstraps and got to work. I had to more or less rebuild it from scratch. That meant knocking down walls and reorganising rooms so I could see the sea and sky from every single corner – that mattered to me more than anything else. I could see them from the bath, the bed, all the living spaces.

Ages ago, when a cabin at the end of the world was only a dream, I'd made a mental list of what I really wanted in my next home, and right at the top of that list was a beautiful old bath that I could lie in and look out at water. So when I was redoing the layout, the tub was one of the first things I found a spot for. I've also always loved the idea of a window seat, and had to make one somewhere in the shack – as the place is so small, there had to be a lot of doubling up, so sometimes it's a window seat, sometimes it's a couch and it's also a bed every now and then.

With every decision I made, I was really conscious of the shack's history – it's part of a group built out of recycled materials by local miners and railway workers early last century. Over the years, the shacks have evolved in fairly haphazard style, which only makes them even more special.

I replaced the aluminium windows with recycled ones, which still have the old glass in them, so the view is a little bit wonky, which I love. Some people had tried to convince me to put new glass in, but I knew that would be wrong.

I changed the sliding doors for some lovely old French doors that had been for sale for ages – the woman who used to own them wanted to be sure they were going to a good home, and came to see where I wanted to put them. I had to beg her to sell them to me, and thankfully she did. I made a new kitchen that works for me – it's simple, and I can make a mess in it, and then just hide everything away in the sink when I've finished.

My budget for Captains Rest was tiny – almost everything in it came from junk shops or, importantly, from people I love. I did things like turning an old desk into a sink unit in the bathroom – it was a lot of work to do, but was totally worth it. It's always going to be there now. I'd found a pair of children's beds that had been handmade years ago for twin boys. I was desperate to use them in the shack, so ended up joining the headboards together to make one big bed. Again, that took months to do, but there's so much story attached to it now – it's so beautiful to me that the boys will always be together.

This place will always be a safe harbour. Through creating it, in a way, it created me. My work, my life in that town I wasn't fond of, and the marriage I felt the same way about, came to an end. A new chapter started for me – with Captains Rest came a new life. A new place to call home, new work helping others create the same – and new love. I sometimes think of this little place as a bag of magic beans, trading wishes. I will be forever grateful.

I thought I'd spend my life on the ocean, sailing alone on a boat full of mahogany and red velvet, lit by oil lamps and guided by the stars. But it didn't happen, and every encounter on dry land always seemed like a collision until I found a little shack in Tasmania. I'm the captain and she's my rest.

I like to tell stories in everything around me. Maybe I'm a bit of a dreamer, and definitely a romantic. I've always lived in a world that's different from everyone else's, and one that I've created myself. I love old and found, gifted and treasured things.

Looking out to sea first thing in the morning, I can tell if I'm going to be having fish for breakfast or not. If I do, some of the little buoys will be underwater, heavy with a fat salmon, escaped from one of the fish farms. I'll row over in my boat and retrieve my catch, and bring it back to cook at home.

148

Besides fishing adventures, there's sitting, reading, sunning, walking,
painting, writing, dreaming, bathing and sleeping. Mostly to bird song
and piano music, lit by pink skies and rainbows, candles and stars.

The perfect day tends to happen to me every day here. I wake up with pretty pink skies bouncing around the giant mirror the seas make. All the birds are calling my name, most of all my four little ducks who wait patiently at my door for breakfast.

You know that feeling when you were a kid of going to your nan's house (it was a nan for me, she was English and so elegant). You'd have your own bedroom, the sheets would always feel the same, and the house had its own lovely smell. At mine, we would have strawberries and cream every night for dessert while we watched *Neighbours*, and there would always be a glass of water with a napkin over it next to my bed every night. They are such beautiful memories – I hope everyone has a few of their own that make them feel like this.

I get reminded of these feelings when I stay at Captains Cottage, a tiny little cottage that I consider to be one of my second homes. I stay there whenever I'm in Hobart, which is pretty often, and as soon as I walk in the door, it feels like a homecoming. I love that. I travel so much and it's still a rare feeling.

This little place was one of my first styling jobs after I'd finished Captains Rest. Kylie, its gorgeous owner, got in touch with me out of the blue to see if I could help – she and her husband, Sean, lived up in Brisbane and had bought the house online, and wanted to rent it out as soon as they could. I was going to France four days later, so had to pull the whole thing together in no time; I remember having a meeting with her while I was sitting in my parked car by the side of a road – it was all very last minute, but there's a thrill in that. Chance, I suppose. The house was virtually empty the first time I saw it, but it was still a gorgeous little place, so humble and real, even though it had been mucked up over the years with carpet, whitewash and paint. Kylie wanted me to bring it back to life, and I could tell immediately what needed to be done to it.

It's an actual ship captain's house, built in the middle of the 1800s, and really, like all houses do, it told me what it wanted to be. I called it the Captains Cottage straightaway, and the name stuck. The only direction to go was to turn it back to a house you could imagine the sea captain living in. Or, how I often like to think about things – me, as that sea captain.

Kylie had the basic furniture, and not too much else – part of my job was to get hold of the rest of the furniture and other bits and pieces for the house.

That meant mapping out what was needed to make it functional – a desk, rugs, cushions, all sorts of things. The budget, I have to say, was tiny, but that was fine – Hobart is so full of little shops where, as long as you don't mind getting your hands dirty, you can rummage through boxes and find amazing things for almost nothing. Kylie more or less left me to it – she said she completely trusted me, which was incredible, but also incredibly nice, seeing at that time we hadn't even met.

I'd send her photos every day so she could see what I'd bought. One of my best finds was at the tip shop in South Hobart, where I picked up a whole stack of beautiful little paintings for a dollar each. I was looking high and low for rope to wind into a light fitting – I ended up talking to a man in an antique shop, and he went out the back and there was some lying in his garden, disintegrating. I paid him five dollars for the lot. Then there was an old model boat that was so broken I got it for nothing – surrounded by maritime books I'd found and a vase of flowers that I'd picked from the verges by the side of the road, it suddenly looked really beautiful.

Once you've worked out what the story of a house is – in this case, who the sea captain was and how he would have passed the time in his little cottage – it's a matter of finding pieces that fit with that. It's about creating loose collections of things in the right colours, that tell the right tale, that form a bit of a tapestry. It's so much fun to get lost in that imaginary world. I'm sure the captain would have picked up lots of bits of flotsam and jetsam himself – not everything would have been new and perfect in his day. That means I was not looking for things that were made at about the same time the house was built – it was more important they had the right feel for him, whatever age they might be.

Somehow or other, I managed to finish everything before I went off to France. It's gone on to be such an iconic short stay in Hobart; it makes me really happy that other people, too, have had a chance to experience it and love this place as much as I do. It's also good to know that even though I might have helped Kylie and Sean at the beginning, they've gone on to make it their own – they haven't changed anything I did, but every time I go, they've put a little bit more of themselves into the house, which might mean changing the basic cutlery for antiques, and more like the captain might use himself.

The best thing about Captains Cottage to me is that it's so humble, but so powerful – the feeling of being there is just so beautiful. It's not about what it costs, it's about how it feels.

You can let your imagination fly when you create story; to me, the captain was a big reader whose favourite books were waiting for him when he came on shore leave.
A little bit like myself.

CAPTAINS COTTAGE

Captains Cottage, although small, is such a beautiful house to be in. It is now a full-time hosted home and it's magical to watch so many other people enjoy the space in the way I intended.

Small moments, such as this little arrangement on the mantelpiece, make Captains Cottage memorable and a place I want to keep returning to.

CAPTAINS COTTAGE

My job was to bring life to the cottage, finding objects to work with the furniture that was already there, like this table and chair set.

CAPTAINS COTTAGE

It could have been tempting to paint the timber wall, but I'm sure the captain would have approved leaving it as it is. Age should always be celebrated!

THE NUN'S ROOM

The Nun's Room was where my interest in spaces started. Quite seriously, I've been decorating and renovating this little house since I was five. This tiny place has been mine since my family moved into a property in Geraldton on the coast in Western Australia. It's the original house on the property, built by immigrant farmers – basically one room with a few flimsy partitions in it. To get to it, you have to walk through the yard behind the main house, around a pool and through a few gates. As soon as my parents let me have it, I began to think about how I wanted to use it and how to make it my own. It really was the beginning of understanding that we can all create our own world around us. I wanted to create a space to live in, away from the noise and chaos and visual clutter of a home full of love, but also a younger sister and brother.

Even as a little kid, I used to spend days in here alone, in silence, reading, thinking, imagining what was going to happen in my life one day. And that's how my dad came up with the name, the Nun's Room. It was a joke at first, me as a little nun, which is not far from the truth, but it has always stuck. In my case, though, I'd constantly have my nose in a book, or be dreaming of adventure and escape.

It has been a sanctuary for me all through my life, evolving to suit me. I moved in when I was a teenager, only going back to the main house for meals and to use Mum and Dad's bathroom. The Nun's Room would be full of candles and love letters, and there would still be stacks of books. Years later, when I came back from Mexico, I lived here again for a while. It was a place of calm, as it was after my marriage ended – the third time in my life I had to pack it all up and move back home.

I filled it with pieces I'd picked up all over the place – things my parents no longer had any use for, bits and pieces from op shops and, later, ones I'd found on my travels. Over the years, things got shipped in and out, so the mood of it constantly shifted as well. It was in this room that I worked out that I didn't like plain walls of just plasterboard and paint. My mother and I wallpapered the space together, even doing the ceiling in the bedroom until we realised that was too difficult, and left it. It's paintable paper, so even that's very easy to change.

Given it's on the other side of the country, I don't spend much time in the Nun's Room anymore, but it's still well used by cousins and nieces and nephews passing through. My youngest niece was in there recently, and when Mum asked her what she was doing, she said, 'Smelling Auntie Sarah.' I just thought that was so special. I know I'll never forget it.

THE NUN'S ROOM

The Nun's Room has always been a place to escape to, and where I can dream and experiment. It's had so many lives alongside mine in the time I have lived there.

THE NUN'S ROOM

I love dark and textured walls for small spaces. They recede, and make the spaces feel so much bigger. The secret is finishing the ceilings to match the walls.

THE NUN'S ROOM

The mood was always changing in the Nun's Room as things got shipped in and out.
In such a small space, every item is considered, and changed with the seasons.

THE NUN'S ROOM

Reminders of the sea always found their way in there, preferably en masse.
Collections are so important for spaces that tell my stories.

I met Emma when she came to my hosting school, The Hosting Masterclass. She got in touch with me soon after and asked if I'd be interested in helping her and her husband, Stuart, with Ethelmont Rise. It sounded like my favourite kind of job – they were happy to do the work; they just needed me to give them some direction.

I went round to see them, and they're such a gorgeous family. Their house is on a cul-de-sac in Sandy Bay in Hobart. It's the sort of street where residents plant flowers in the verges. Ethelmont Rise is nestled in, with views of the water where boats are bobbing around all day long.

It's an Arts and Crafts-style house from the 1920s that had last been modernised in the eighties. Before Emma and Stuart bought it, it had been rented out. The only original things left were two incredible yellow velvet ceiling lamps, which I knew had to stay – everything else could go.

A couple of unmarried sisters were the first people to live in the house, and the idea of that sounded so eccentric. I could never live with my sister, as much as I adore her. You get a sense for a house when you're in it, and you can tell that the sisters loved being there together, happy in each other's company and not having much to do with anyone else around them. All the windows have big ledges, and it's easy to imagine them sitting there doing their needlework, looking out to the river and gossiping about the neighbours.

When I was putting together my ideas, I kept thinking about the two women. I gave Emma and Stuart two options, but one was a bit more decorative. It was going to depend on their comfort level, and luckily they went with the darker, more atmospheric scheme, more the sort of place I could picture the sisters in.

Using those ideas as our compass, Emma and Stuart would find furniture and other bits and pieces and send snaps to me for a tick or a cross. Emma has a great eye – she did a lot of shopping on eBay and Gumtree and in antique shops, and we'd go through them together to see what would work. She and Stuart had already bought some things such as bathroom fittings before I got involved, and they had found the kitchen cabinets on Gumtree. We didn't want a plain wall in the house – to me, there's nothing more uninspiring than flat paint, so each wall is either lime washed with Porter's Paints, tiled or papered. Emma chose wallpapers and wall colours, using the parameters I had given them to work within.

Near the end, we found the boat and the owl, which Emma called Harry Swoop. I love the character they bring.

This is another house I've spent some time in. Soon after we finished, the pandemic hit, and I moved in for a while. It was such a lovely place to be while the world felt so uncertain. Although it feels as if you're walking into the sisters' house, there's nothing at all dowdy about it. It was also a happy collaboration – Emma and Stuart worked hard, and it feels special to have been a part of bringing this home to life.

ETHELMONT RISE

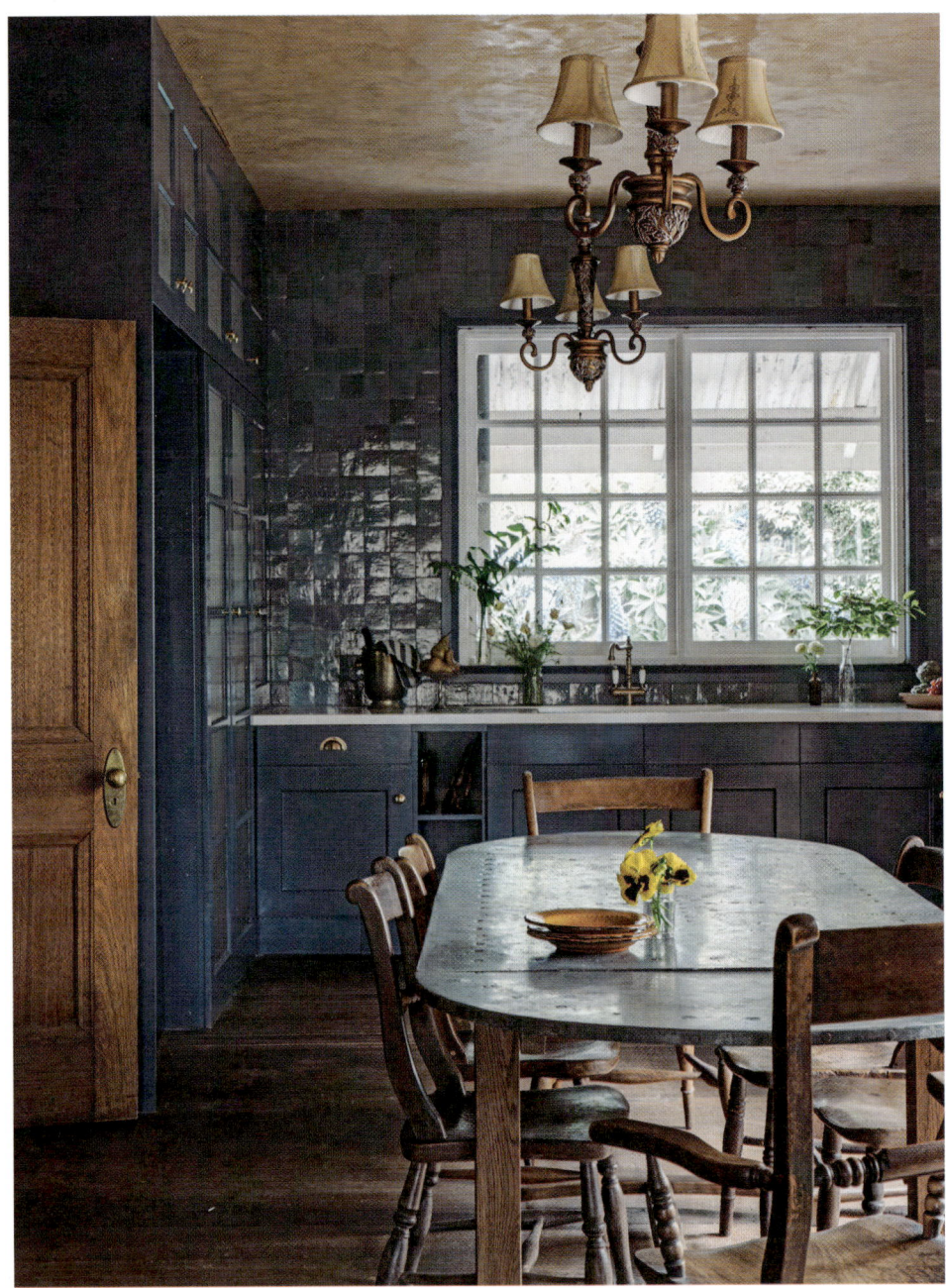

I'm all for reusing where you can – Emma and Stuart found the kitchen cabinets, originally cream, on Gumtree and painted them blue. Reduce, reuse, restore – as well as the right thing to do, it adds a charm that can't be bought off the shelf.

I can still picture the two sisters in Ethelmont Rise, doing what they've always done – drinking tea and gossiping about the neighbours. If I lived here with my sister, that's what we would be doing too.

For homes with old stories, I always love old portraits in unexpected places.
It feels as if the homes have changed around where the stories have always been.

The secret to shelves is 1. More than books, tell your stories.
2. Always place in unexpected ways. 3. Collate colour.

PART THREE

10 Rooms

It's time now to show you ten rooms that work for me, and explain to you why. Part magic, but mostly science and story – these are rooms I think about and reference often when explaining the principles of style to my own students – examples that get an A+ from me. Explore them with an eye to what you've learnt so far.

ROOM 1

LE MOULIN BRÉGEON

Linières-Bouton, France

This section of a bathroom in a converted watermill in the Loire Valley is one of the most decadent and delicious rooms I could ever imagine myself starting or ending the day in. It tells enough story to capture me – so much so this is a space I can't forget.

It has so much going on it, but the fact that it's so balanced and has been so carefully considered means that, overall, there's a great sense of calm. The triangular shape of the ceiling is echoed in the placement of the lovely mix of objects, all useful for bathing, within the room – the mirrors at either end of the bench forming the base of the triangle with the painting above the window its apex. And there's another triangle made up of the window with the framed photos on either side. The strong lines of beams are counterbalanced by all the circles – the mirrors, the window, some of the framed photographs – and, as in many of my favourite rooms, a variety of textures can be found. There's the marble top of the timber cabinet; the cotton rugs on the tiles; metal and ceramics; the soft wash on the walls against the tiled floor. The placement of the beautiful nude is inspired and totally unexpected – what perfect company in this gorgeous space.

ROOM 2

LA FUSTAIA

Sarzana, Italy

The first thing I noticed about this bedroom in a former Italian hunting lodge was the blue-grey panelling. It's so unusual to see the same colour used for walls, doors, architraves, everything. Here, the intensely velvety shade, so velvety I want to touch it, creates a really beautiful backdrop for the fireplace, for the the forest outside and for the rest it inspires. Touches of that grey find their way into the rest of the room, adding up to a real sense of harmony. There's probably a bathroom behind that door, but it takes you a moment to even notice it's there. Everything that can be hidden is. I love that for a bedroom – nothing to distract you from the task you are there to do. There's a lovely mix of textures here – the gilded picture frame, the contemporary metal lamp, the extravagant bed linen, the upholstery on the chair, even the dried branches in the fireplace. It's perfectly intentional without feeling stiff. The mix of objects from different times and places is so particular and so deliberate, and completely unforgettable. This is a room that has no problem passing my eyelash test – if you look at it with your eyes almost closed, there's nothing jarring, and nothing leaps out. This room, for me, is a lesson for you in less. Feel brave in your pursuit of creating rooms that nudge you in the direction of what you are there to do.

ROOM 3

CAMELLAS-LLORET

Montréal, France

Please never feel you need much budget at all to decorate and tell your stories; what you need to have is your own sense of who you are – that's the main thing the room in this rustic garden apartment shows. You can just tell they've used things they've treasured – the drawings of herbs on paper are almost all you need in here. The way they've hung them is so powerful – if they were spaced out around the room, which is how you'd expect to see them, they'd really lose their impact. It also shows that beauty comes from imperfection – the lampshade's a bit wonky and the paintwork's slightly chipped. Then there are those beams, and the texture of the terracotta tiles. Against all that is the circular table with its shiny top and a mixture of chairs and stools around it. Again, that mix of circles – in the table, stool and lampshade – soften the grid of the flooring and the herb drawings. Can you try and imagine this room with a square table? It wouldn't feel as beautiful, would it. That is the power of a curve for you! Again, the power of restraint in this room amplifies its beautiful voice.

ROOM 4

FOLLONICO

Montefollonico, Italy

What I love about this bedroom in Tuscany, created from a space where the original farmhouse kitchen used to be, is its perfect sense of balance and texture. The rustic doors above the bed juxtaposed against the circular frames massed together above the couch. The rich red velvet and fringing of the couch against the simple bed linen. The contemporary metal standard lamp alongside the metal elements on the rustic doors. The dark timber beams balanced by the oversized floor tiles. Textures combine in interesting ways – the timber of the old doors; bedside tables made of tree trunks; the slightly rough timber bed frame. Velvet and metal; timber and tile – if you looked at each of those elements separately, you wouldn't necessarily think they would work together, but in the right proportions they do. I wanted to show you this room to teach you a sense of proportion and consideration. Thinking about the right things for your space in terms of its story, its use, texture and balance before you rush out and find or buy a lot of things, the things everyone else has, or the things you think you should. Slowing the process down and placing with intention that comes from you.

ROOM 5

MAISON EMPEREUR

Marseille, France

This bedroom is a fairytale to me, and I've always wanted to be in a fairytale – I think we all should get that chance if we want it. It's above one of the oldest hardware shops in France, and is furnished with pieces from the family archives. It's hard to imagine a more genuine story than that. But beyond that, it's a perfect lesson in texture and layering – the untreated timber bed and table on the highly polished concrete floors; the linen pillows contrasting with the well-worn upholstery on the bedside chair; the slightly ornate standard lamp begging for a shade, but so much better without; the bleached timber bedstead set against the deep tobacco walls. Think about geometry I taught you and you'll be able to see a triangles in this space, formed by the chair, cupboard and bed, and providing balance to the lamp on the other side of the room. There are plenty of straight lines here – the bed, cupboard, table and chair – but to soften those, circles can be seen in the shade overhead, the decorative elements on the bedposts, the bedside lamp. This room doesn't need artwork – that wall cabinet is an installation in itself.

ROOM 6

WORMISTOUNE

Crail, Scotland

Wormistoune is one of my favourite places on earth. I was lucky enough to get the chance to spend a little of my winter there one year, and while I know we are all supposed to stay present, I find my thoughts drift back to this place often – and the people that make this place so special to me. It's in Fife, in Scotland, and is the spiritual home of the Scottish wyrm, a dragon-like serpent allegedly slain by a medieval knight. I learnt this story, alongside so many others about witches and townspeople and lairds and ladies and the history of Scotland – there's just so much story attached to Wormistoune, and you can feel that sense of all of time echoing in every bit of panelling, every door and window, every hallway, every room. Scottish history is both glorious and dark, and it's impossible to be here without thinking of what has happened in this place over the centuries. It's felt, and I am so grateful its owners embraced and rejoiced in all of it, bringing this place back to life, instead of installing anything modern. In this cosy snug, there's layer upon layer of texture – it's not enough to have the family tartan on the couch when you can use it for the flooring as well, which is an unexpectedly extravagant detail. I swear I'll never forget the bathroom at Wormistoune with its custom tartan floor – I remember feeling at the time that it was tartan, not tile, that would be the future of bathrooms for me.

ROOM 7

HÔTEL DE TINGRY

Ménerbes, France

There's something so lovely about this room in Provence – its incredible scale and that wallcovering make me feel envious – we just don't have access to such grandeur here where I live in the Southern Hemisphere.

If you look carefully, using my rules as a guide, this room has it all. There's colour and texture and story and the use of circles. It's so obvious that they've just chosen colours they love, or used things that they already have, and haven't overthought anything – who else would put the curtains and wallpaper together. It wouldn't work in a lot of places, but here it really does. The texture here comes from age, which is another sign of story – the faded fabric, the worn tiles and mirror frame and, on the fireplace, the remnants of thousands of fires. In my ten rules, I say that circles speak of life, and that's true here – the lampshade, the basket with firewood, the candle, the wallpaper design, the turn of the chair leg, the vaulted ceiling and the mouldings on the mirror frame all give a softness to the scene and help make us feel human. And also make us all feel like moving to France.

ROOM 8

NAPIER QUARTER

Fitzroy, Australia

Daniel, the owner of this magical apartment you can stay in next to his restaurant, is a student and friend of mine. I have so many happy and wine-hazed memories of this perfectly lit and styled space I like to stay at every time I am in Melbourne. This is about not doing too much – having a few beautiful things, the right things, arranging them properly and then leaving them alone so you can put your own life in its shoes, so to speak. Again, it's about circles and curves and the way they make us immediately feel comfortable and safe somehow – the archway leading to the hallway, the banister and timber chair backs, the amazing metal shade, the corners of the table, the wooden tray the masses of lemons are in and even the nude in the painting. Daniel has an exquisite eye. He buys things he loves from people he admires and they are celebrated in his spaces. You just find the right things and don't need to do anything else. 'Stella', who you can see here, has a sister painting 'Vivienne' who lives upstairs. The lemons come from a local grower friend, and the honey in the kitchen next door is from the bees that pollinated them. This is a lesson in knowing your story and executing it perfectly.

ROOM 9

STELOR

Gotlands Tofta, Sweden

I dream of Stelor. I've included it in this book in the hope I might be able to visit one day and become part of the family forever. Is that cheeky!? But in all seriousness, I've included them because the spaces are not hotel squeaky, they're just perfect. The relaxed nature of this particular room is really welcoming – the chairs that are so obviously well used and well loved, the pipes at ceiling level (anyone else would try to hide them), the seriously non-matching furniture and its seemingly haphazard arrangement. Each piece adds to the story, and helps give the room its sense of character. Texture plays a big part in the success of this room – the worn leather, the whitewashed walls, the graphic rug and the lacquer-like finish on the little chest of drawers, and so too does the use of circles in all their different forms, such as the curvaceous chairs, the candlestick, the standard lamp and garland decoration on the chest, offset by the very obvious straight lines in the flooring and rug.

ROOM 10

DUNMORE FARM

Molyullah, Australia

The dining area at Dunmore Farm, in north-eastern Victoria, speaks to picking things you genuinely love without worrying too much about what should be there. What they've done here is chosen everything to fit with their story and aesthetics without any hang-ups about what they should be doing. Which I love. I don't know where we all got so lost in doing the expected in spaces instead of what we love and find useful. A lot of people putting this room together would think they needed to put a big piece of art on the end wall, or they'd have a bigger table with a tablecloth on it, and put it in the middle of the room. It's perfectly balanced the way it is with a lovely mix of circles and straight lines – the dining chairs (it's better that they don't all match) and that amazing overhead light with its coiled cord. This is another room that passes my eyelash test – they've stripped out all the colours, and it just feels so calm and humble and right. It's such a beautiful space. What is beauty? What's real is beautiful, I think, and what is beautiful is real.

PLACES

Albert and Grace,
Boonah, Australia
@albertandgrace_shop

Camellas-Lloret,
Montréal, France
@camellaslloret
camellaslloret.com

Captains Cottage,
Hobart, Tasmania
@captainscottagehobart
captainscottagehobart.com

Captains Rest,
Lettes Bay, Tasmania
@captainsrest
captainsrest.com

Château de Dirac, Dirac, France
@chateaudedirac
lespetitesemplettes.com

Château d'Uzer, Uzer, France
@chateauduzer
chateau-uzer.com

Dunmore Farm,
Molyullah, Australia
@dunmore_farm
www.dunmorefarm.com.au

Ethelmont Rise,
Sandy Bay, Tasmania
@ethelmontrise

Ewing Farm, Tylden, Australia
@ewingfarm

Follonico, Montefollonico, Italy
@follonico_
follonico.com

Hôtel de Tingry,
Ménerbes, France
@lamaisondoramaar
maisondoramaar.org

La Belle Vue, Neffiès, France
@labellevueneffies
labellevue.se

La Fustaia, Sarzana, Italy
@lafustaiasarzana
lafustaia.it

Le Moulin Brégeon,
Linières-Bouton, France
@lemoulinbregeon
moulinbregeon.com

L'épicerie de Vénat,
Saint-Yrieix-sur-Charente,
France
@lepicerie_de_venat
lepicerie-de-venat.com

Locanda del Loggiato,
Bagno Vignoni, Italy
@lemarinihospitality
loggiato.it

Lucy's Lane,
Port Fairy, Australia
@lucyslaneportfairy

Maison Bergogne,
Narrowsburg, USA
@maisonbergogne
maisonbergogne.com

Maison Empereur,
Marseille, France
@maisonempereur
empereur.fr

My Sister & The Sea,
Marion Bay, Australia
@mysisterandthesea
mysisterandthesea.com

Napier Quarter,
Fitzroy, Australia
@napier_quarter
napierquarter.com.au

Numeroventi, Florence, Italy
@_numeroventi_
numeroventi.it

Ship Inn, Stanley, Australia
@shipinnstanley
shipinnstanley.com.au

Smokey Belles, Narrowsburg, USA
@smokeybellescatskills

Steam, Forrest, Australia
dufflebird.com.au

Stelor, Gotlands Tofta, Sweden
stelor.se

The Butcher's House,
Bothwell, Australia
bothwellbutchershouse.com

The Cottage,
Kangaroo Valley, Australia
@thecottagekangaroovalley
thecottagekangaroovalley.com

The Oxford,
Hepburn Springs, Australia
@thehousesdaylesford
thehousesdaylesford.com

The Waterfront House,
Erowal Bay, Australia

Valdirose, Lastra a Signa, Italy
@valdirose
valdirose.com

Villa Pienza, Pienza, Italy
@villapienza
villapienza.it

Villa 61, Limana, Italy
@villa61.it
villa61.it

Wormistoune, Crail, Scotland
@wormistoune
wormistoune.com

PEOPLE

Aurélie Alvarez
@aurelie.alvarez1
aureliealvarez.com

Sibella Court
@sibellacourt
thesocietyinc.com.au

Geoffrey Preston
@geoffreyprestonsculpture
geoffreypreston.co.uk

PHOTOGRAPHERS

Antonella Machet
@slowlivinghideaway
slowlivinghideaway.com
Pages: 10, 11, 12, 13, 20, 21, 24, 25, 36, 37, 46, 47, 58, 59, 60, 61, 80, 84, 85, 86, 87, 92, 93, 94, 98, 99, 106, 107, 110, 118, 119, 120, 121, 126, 127, 130, 131, 132, 133, 191, 193, 195, 197, 199

Marnie Hawson
@marniehawson
marniehawson.com.au
Pages: 6, 14, 15, 16, 26-27, 48, 49, 50, 51, 52, 53, 70, 71, 72-73, 88-89, 100-101, 102, 103, 104-105, 114, 115, 139, 140-141, 142-143, 144, 145, 146, 147, 148, 149, 150, 151, 155, 156-157, 158-159, 160, 161, 162, 163, 174, 176-177, 178, 179, 180-181, 182, 183, 184-185, 186, 187, 209

Jessica Tremp
@jessicatremp
jessicatremp.bigcartel.com
Pages: ii, vi, vii, 8, 9, 18, 19, 30, 31, 42, 43, 56, 57, 68, 69, 82, 83, 96, 97, 112, 113, 124, 125, 212, 214

Sarah Andrews
@sarahandrews.co
sarahandrews.co
Pages: 22, 23, 62, 63, 90, 91, 136, 152, 164, 166, 167, 168, 169, 170, 171, 172, 173

Alexander Baxter
@alexbaxter.co
alexbaxter.co
Pages: 66, 76, 77, 78-79, 201

Nick Carter
@nickcarterphotography
Page: 28

Sibella Court
@sibellacourt
thesocietyinc.com.au
Pages: 54, 65

Peter Crosby
@pbcrosby
petercrosbyphotography.com
Pages: 38, 39, 74, 75

Kristoffer Paulsen
@kristofferpaulsen
kristofferpaulsen.com
Pages: 108-109, 205

Ruth Ribeaucourt
@ruthribeaucourt
thefrenchmuse.com
Pages: 40, 44, 45, 122, 128, 129, 203

Lean Timms
@leantimms
leantimms.com
Pages: 32-33, 34, 35, 116-117, 207

Mikkel Vang
@vangsterama
mikkelvang.com
Page: 64

ABOUT THE AUTHOR

Sarah Andrews is a scientist, designer and teacher. Her unique background brings structured processes and original ideas to interior arts and design, which she has used to educate thousands of students around the world in her online school and in-person masterclasses. She is well-known for creating and teaching timeless, iconic and authentic interiors across personal styles, with an enormous number of her students having work appear in publications worldwide. The success of so many of her students has led to her school quickly gaining cult status and international recognition. She lives in a remote part of Tasmania on the sea, and can be found online at @thehostingmasterclass, @sarahandrews.co and @captainsrest.

ACKNOWLEDGEMENTS

Julie Gibbs, Leta Keens, Evi O, Wilson Leung, Lindsey Bro, Simon & Schuster, Marnie Hawson, Antonella Machet, Paige Anderson and Jessica Tremp – this book is in the world because of you. And to Amanda Starkey, Mimi Knoop, Benitha Vlok, Cheryl Carr, Nick Jaffe and the Andrews family – without you, I know my wider work would not exist either. To the photographers and owners who trusted me enough to be showcased in this book, thank you so much. You are all so talented, generous and uniquely you – which is the most magical thing I can think of being. And most importantly, to every student I have ever taught – you know who you are if you are reading this! I am endlessly grateful for you and enamoured of you. You have each shown me the depths and widths of beauty that every single one of us on the planet is capable of, inside our houses and beyond. Thank you – you are so special.

PRINCIPLES OF STYLE

First published in Australia in 2021 by
Simon & Schuster (Australia) Pty Limited
Level 4, 32 York Street, Sydney, NSW 2000

10 9 8 7 6 5 4 3 2

New York Amsterdam/Antwerp London Toronto Sydney New Delhi
Visit our website at www.simonandschuster.com.au

© Sarah Andrews 2021
Photography © Antonella Machet, Marnie Hawson, Jessica Tremp, Sarah Andrews,
Alexander Baxter, Nick Carter, Sibella Court, Peter Crosby, Kristoffer Paulsen,
Ruth Ribeaucourt, Lean Timms, Mikkel Vang

All rights reserved. No part of this publication may be reproduced, stored in a retrieval system,
or transmitted in any form or by any means, electronic, mechanical, photocopying,
recording or otherwise, without prior permission of the publisher.

A catalogue record for this book is available from the National Library of Australia

ISBN: 9781761102714

Cover image: Jessica Tremp
Cover and internal design: Evi O. Studio
Printed and bound in China by RR Donnelley

MIX
Paper | Supporting responsible forestry
FSC® C144853